YES
YOU CAN RAISE HAPPY RESPONSIBLE CHILDREN

Simple Solutions and Real-Life Examples
for Successful Parenting.

Martha A. Burich, M.Ed

First published by Ultimate World Publishing 2024
Copyright © 2024 Martha Burich

ISBN

Paperback: 978-1-923255-30-2
Ebook: 978-1-923255-31-9

Martha Burich has asserted her rights under the Copyright, Designs and Patents Act 1988 to be identified as the author of this work. The information in this book is based on the author's experiences and opinions. The publisher specifically disclaims responsibility for any adverse consequences which may result from use of the information contained herein. Permission to use information has been sought by the author. Any breaches will be rectified in further editions of the book.

All rights reserved. No part of this publication may be reproduced, stored in or introduced into a retrieval system, or transmitted in any form, or by any means (electronic, mechanical, photocopying, recording or otherwise) without the prior written permission of the author. Any person who does any unauthorised act in relation to this publication may be liable to criminal prosecution and civil claims for damages. Enquiries should be made through the publisher.

Cover design: Ultimate World Publishing
Layout and typesetting: Ultimate World Publishing
Editor: Alex Floyd-Douglass

Ultimate World Publishing
Diamond Creek,
Victoria Australia 3089
www.writeabook.com.au

Testimonials

A practical and easy to understand guide for all parents. This book is a MUST for your family.

Lynn Lowrance Ed.D
Counselor and Parent Educator

This book is a practical and easy to read parenting guide. It's especially helpful for parents of children 18 months to six years of age as they navigate the child's rapid growth and brain development. The organized chapters are like having the parenting advice of a wise senior family member right at your fingertips.

Debbie Sluys, Founder, Director, CEO at Dare to Declare Academy, Former Director at Growing Together Family Resource Centre.

I love this book. It is engaging and easy to read. Martha shares many practical parenting tips to help children feel loved and happy. Parenting is a fluid experience, and this book helps parents navigate it.

Pamela Gail Johnson
Founder-Society of Happy People, Speaker and Author of *Practical Happiness: Four Principles to Improve Your Life*

With practical advice and great parenting insights, this book offers effective strategies for parenting children. It is an essential resource for parents looking to inspire and support their children's development and behavior.

Shelly Pawelko
Shelly Marie Thrive Academy

It's been often quoted, "If only children came with a manual." This is that manual. As an educational colleague of hers, I witnessed and participated in her approach to working with children. In the classroom, her lessons were always engaging and her creativity kept it fun for the students. Her book is succinct, yet impactful, giving parents a perfect blueprint for guiding children as they navigate their childhoods. Gems like "As soon as you..." instead of "If". A constant infusion of positive reinforcement and enrichment activities abound in this work. Martha's background in Psychology and Education has served her well! I would recommend anyone embarking on the frontier that is parenthood to read and learn from the sound practices infused with wisdom and common sense she offers within. She is excellence personified.

Jacqueline Hanna Martin,
Educator, 42 yrs. Retired

Between these pages will be found empowering methods of communicating with your child that will increase the opportunity for healthy self-esteem development. As a parent, try blending several of these methods on a weekly basis until they feel a normal part of your communication style.

Dennis LaMacchia MS
Experienced Counsellor.Teacher.Administrator.

A short read that is practical and easy to understand with good answers and examples to raise smart and responsible children. It is in my favorite style, numbered steps, making this difficult job manageable—one, two, three, it's that easy! The summary is a great checklist to remember and go back to. Highly recommend for parents, grandparents, teachers, care givers and anyone who spends time with children.

Kathy Velloff
Bachelors of Science in Education Masters of Education in Library Science
School Librarian, 25yrs.
Retired

A fantastic, much needed book. It is clear and gives good, practical advice. Most of all, it helps parents develop well adjusted, confident young people who focus on the positive.

Patricia Kennedy Founder:
Body Mindset Connection.

I dedicate this book to:

Anthony Burich, my son and teacher.

My Mother (Margaret Nardoni Johnson Kruse 1919-2009)

My family in Valle Corsa, Italy: Nardoni, Colagiovanni, Colandrea, Cimaroli.

My Father (Edward Francis Johnson 1916-1994).

My family in Boston MA and Scotland: Johnson

My husband (Anthony Wendel Burich 1956-2008)

My family in Croatia: Simich and Burich.

OTHER PRODUCTS BY MARTHA BURICH

BOOKS:

Chicken Soup for the Soul Cookbook. Contributing Author.

Interviewed for *Practical Happiness: Four Principles to Improve Your Life* (HCI) by Pamela Gail Johnson.

Yes You Can Teach Them All (Author, Publication 2025).

WEB

Youtube:
www.youtube.com/@learningmore727/videos
www.youtube.com/@marthaburich/videos

Online Parenting Classes and Workshops:
marthaburich.com

Facebook Group:
Yes You Can Raise Happy Responsible Children FaceBook Group

If I were to search for the central core of difficulties in people, as I have come to know them, it is that in a great majority of cases they despise themselves, regarding themselves as worthless and unlovable.

Dr. Carl Rogers

Contents

Testimonials	iii
Introduction	1
Building Self-Esteem	3
Discipline	9
Creating Positive Relationships with Your Children	15
Raising Smart Children	19
Mealtimes	25
At the Grocery Store	29
Travel: Across the Street or Across the Country	35
Creating a Safe Home	39
To Strengthen Your Marriage	43
Praise and Encouragement	51
About The Author	55
Resources	57
Offers	59

Introduction

Raising happy, intelligent children is no more complicated than understanding the fundamentals of self-esteem. Because self-esteem is so important to success in life, we know that when we use parenting techniques based upon its principles, we cannot fail to raise responsible, loving children who care about themselves and the world in which they live.

Although many parents and educators speak of the importance of self-esteem, when it comes down to it, they continue to use the discipline and communication techniques that have caused too many children to grow up feeling inadequate and inferior.

We are not taught that with self-esteem we have limitless potential, or that this power is at our disposal and can be used to work miracles in our lives and the lives of our children.

Yes, You Can

As parents, we want joyful relationships with our children, and we want to give them the best foundation upon which to build the rest of their lives. However, often we come to parenting armed with little of the knowledge we need to enable us to confidently handle the many challenges of this tremendous responsibility.

We are not alone.

All too often the very people we look to for guidance in raising our children are no more informed than we are.

The good news is there is information available to help us make effective decisions regarding parenting.

To get some new information and other ways of handling your children, turn the page.

Building Self-Esteem

Our level of self-esteem determines how we interact with the people and things around us. When we have low self-esteem, we take failure personally and often refuse to try, rather than risk failure or rejection.

With high self-esteem we have the courage to try and are not discouraged by failure. High self-esteem is built through positive interactions with others along with successful experiences and accomplishments, no matter how small. To build your child's self-esteem, follow these simple tips:

1. Notice the good and say something about it every day such as, *"You picked up your toys. Thanks!"* or *"You are being nice to your sister. I like that."* You could take it a step further and then ask your child, *"How do you feel about that?"* or *"I notice you are doing your homework without being asked. How does that make you*

feel? How is that helping you? What are you learning from that? What results are you getting?" By asking these questions, you help the child internalize their behavior.

2. Give your child choices every day. *"Would you like to wear the red pants or the blue ones? Do you want peanut butter or ham for lunch? Would you like to go to bed at 7 or 7:30?"* Often just having a choice will eliminate a lot of misbehavior. Give them a choice between just two items, though. More than that could be overwhelming, and no choice at all makes children feel powerless.

3. Use your child's interests as the basis for conversation. *"I see you playing with your cars a lot. Do you like them? What do you like about them? How do you make them go so fast?"* or *"What is it about dinosaurs that you like so much?"*

4. Accept your child's feelings and give these feelings a name. *"You seem really happy about that,"* or *"You seem really mad. It can be disappointing when a friend can't come out to play." "I cry at sad movies, too."*

5. Use **AS SOON AS** in place of **IF**: *"As soon as you are dressed, you may watch TV."* If you do nothing else but

Building Self-Esteem

begin to use this one tip, you will find a remarkable increase in positive behavior. Dr. Lynn Clark author of *SOS Help for Parents* calls this *'Grandma's Rule'*.

6. Tell your children you love them every single day.

7. Allow your child to cry. If your child is crying, they have something to cry about. You could be most helpful by simply commenting, *"You feel really sad,"* or *"I can see you really wanted that toy."* Just acknowledging their sadness, anger or disappointment is enough.

8. Give your child opportunities to be successful. Break large tasks into smaller parts and let them help you one part at a time. Examples would be:
    ❖ Pouring already measured flour or milk into the bowl.
    ❖ Helping you stir ingredients together.
    ❖ Pulling up the top sheet on the bed or neatly placing the pillows on top of the made bed.
    ❖ Arranging a few toys on a shelf or the stuffed animals on the bed.

9. Make a positive comment whenever your child completes a task or portion of a task. This encourages the child.

10. Allow your child to say *"NO"* sometimes.

11. Focus on your child's assets, strengths and contributions.

12. Refrain from comparing your child to others. If the comparison is unfavorable, it can hurt your child's feelings. Even if your child is the 'winner' in the comparison, it can cause feelings of superiority and most likely inferiority since the child will rightly assume that they are only worthy of love and attention when they are the best or worst.

13. When you tuck your child into bed at night, take that opportunity to tell them how much you love them and what you like about them. Examples are their jokes, how generous they are, that they work hard to solve problems, their curiosity and their helpfulness. Also tell them that you are glad they are your child. Imagine how a nightly dose of this will build your child's feelings of self-esteem and self-worth.

14. Take a parenting course. Like any other job, parenting requires special skills and knowledge. Be open to acquiring the information and skills that will make you a more effective parent.

15. Talk about and read uplifting information to your child. Some parents I know read stories from the *Chicken Soup for the Soul* series to their children.

16. There are several resources available that you can read or listen to. These include books and videos on *YouTube*.

*It takes **courage** to be a responsible parent.*

Discipline

Discipline, firm limits and rules are requirements for raising healthy, happy, well-adjusted children. Children who are allowed to consistently misbehave become fearful and unhappy.

Fearful because having no limits can be very frightening, and unhappy because they are denied the sense of accomplishment and belonging that come from cooperation and good behavior. To get the best from your child, follow these simple tips:

1. Tell the child what you want. Rather than saying, *"Don't run,"* tell the child, *"Walk."*

2. When a child misbehaves, rather than punish, give them choices: *"If you want to run around and be noisy, go outside to play. If you'll be quiet, you can*

stay in the house." If the child becomes noisy again simply say, *"I see you've decided to play outside."* Then escort them out.

3. Express your disapproval without attacking your child's character. Instead of saying, *"Your toys are all over again! You are so lazy!"* Tell them, *"I don't like it when you leave toys out."*

4. State what you do want: *"I expect you to put your toys away before you go outside."*

5. Use **AS SOON AS** to avoid punishing or bribing: *"**As soon as** you wash your hands you may eat lunch."* If the child doesn't wash their hands, they won't get to eat, or they must wear gloves.

6. Refrain from hitting your children. Most of the time, we punish when what our children really need are better explanations, more information or to be shown how to do something. Hitting not only breaks the bonds of trust between you and your children, but it shows the child that violence is an acceptable way to settle disputes or to make people change their behavior.

Discipline

7. When you say no, mean it! Saying no but changing it to a yes, if the child cries or complains, only teaches your children that you'll relent if they pester you enough.

8. Threaten only if you intend to follow through. Otherwise, you are teaching your children to ignore what you say. Ever heard of 'mother deafness'? This is how it starts.

9. Please don't name call, tease or be sarcastic with your children. These are self-esteem destroyers and have no place in a loving family.

10. Always bring toys, books, paper, crayons etc. something for your child to do everywhere you go – even for very short trips. In fact, have several items in the car or pack a bag and keep it by the door. You never know when you'll get caught in a traffic jam, run into a friend or get stuck in a long line. This one little thing will save you from the frustration, aggravations, and misbehavior you could get from a bored child.

11. Give your child his wishes in fantasy. Adele Faber and Elaine Mazlish use this example in their book, *How to Talk so Kids Can Listen*.

Child wanted Toasty Crunchies for breakfast but there weren't any in the house.

Child: *"I want Toasty Crunchies for breakfast."*
Mother: *"We don't have any. How about Nifty Crispies?"*
Child: *"No, I hate Nifty Crispies. I want Toasty Crunchies. I want them. I want them."*
Mother: *"I can hear how much you want them. I wish I had a magic wand and could make a giant box appear just for you."*
Child: *"Oh well, I think I'll have some Nifty Crispies."*

Sometimes just acknowledging how much your child wants something will make the reality easier to bear.

12. Two or more times every day, notice what your child is doing that you like, and comment on it or simply describe what you see.

"I like it when you play nicely with your sister."

"You are being quiet, I like that."

"You are being gentle with your books, this keeps them looking new."

Discipline

13. Do your best to anticipate things that will derail your child and remember to tell the child the behavior you do expect.

    When a tantrum does occur distraction is a good course of action. For example, child is having a tantrum at the store you can say: *"I think I just saw a mouse run under that shelf."* or *"I think I saw Barney go to the next isle."* or *"Is this your favorite kind of corn?"*

14. Take a parenting course. It will change your life!

Creating Positive Relationships with Your Children

1. Hug your children often. Hold hands. Smile at them.

2. Notice and comment on what they do right and what you like about them.

3. Encourage them often. To encourage your children, focus on their assets and strengths. This builds self confidence and self-esteem.

4. Give encouragement as they go along – not just for a perfect job or a finished product.

5. Acknowledge their contributions. *"Thank you for picking up the toys, that is such a help to me,"* or *"Thank you for walking next to me, I feel more relaxed at the store when you are near me."*

6. Refrain from using fear to control your children. This only makes them more afraid of the world around them and could cause nightmares. An example I overheard at the store once was, *"John, you stay right here next to Mommy. Otherwise, a bad man could grab you and take you away."* This is too frightening for a small child to handle. You can simply tell the child, *"I feel better when you are near me"* or *"I want you to stay close to me, so I don't have to come looking for you."* If the child won't comply then put him in the cart or go home.

7. Give the child a choice whenever possible. At least once a day, *"Would you like a banana or an apple?"* or *"You can walk next to me or sit in the cart, which do you want?"* Then if the child walks away from you, act. Say, *"I see you've chosen to sit in the cart,"* and put the child in the cart.

8. Talk with enthusiasm about your child's interests. Ask them what they like, don't like and why. Show sincere interest and look at them when talking with them.

Also, please don't ever use something your child has told you against them. This is a terrible breach of trust and could cause your child to decide that it isn't safe to share anything that is really important to them with you in the future.

9. Sarcasm, fault finding, criticism and teasing do not foster positive relations between parents and children. Eliminate these relationship busters from your conversation. Do fun things together. Don't know what your child would like to do? Ask. Make these activities things you both would like to do.

10. Let your child help you with chores. A one-year-old can help fold socks and retrieve easy to reach items. A two-year-old can set spoons, napkins or paper plates on the table. The key is to acknowledge any attempt to do the job right, and to accept a less than perfect outcome. A three-year-old can make a peanut butter and jelly sandwich without making a mess if you'll let him.

11. Ask your child if they want help before you jump in when it looks like they are having difficulty doing something. If they say no, respect their decision.

Raising Smart Children

Most children are not encouraged to use their intellect. As parents, we rob our children of the chances to think for themselves and to learn by doing. We do things for them they can do themselves because we're in too much of a hurry to let the 'slow child' do it themselves.

Instead of asking **them** what they think **they** should do, we tell them what to do. We give advice when we should just listen. We offer solutions when we should ask the child to come up with one of their own.

We waste precious time in the car, in lines, in waiting rooms because we forget to bring something for the child to do or to play with, or we're busy worrying about some problem that won't even matter in a week's time.

Yes, You Can

We intervene in their disputes with siblings and playmates when we would serve them much better by letting **them** work out their own difficulties. We discourage their attempts to help and contribute because the outcome from small hands isn't perfect or 'good enough' for our high adult standards.

We get angry at them when they dare to have opinions different from our own. Then, after all that, we wonder why our children don't seem interested in anything but television, rarely want to try new things, and bother us to do things for them we know they can do for themselves or ask us to solve their problems.

If you want your children to grow to be smart, capable adults, start today to treat them as smart, capable people.

1. Read to your children daily what they want to hear. Research confirms that children who are read to on a regular basis grow to be good readers and better students than those who weren't read to.

2. Let your child read to you. A two-year-old will often memorize a book and read it to you over and over again. Let them.

3. Build on your child's likes. Read the books they like and get books about the toys, subjects and people they like.

4. Encourage any and all efforts your child makes to do and to learn.

5. Explain and show how things work – do this all the time.

6. Ask them to help you so they learn at an early age that they belong and can be of help.

7. Let them help when they want to as often as you can! What they do won't be as perfect as you might like it, but they need these opportunities to learn, and practice improves performance.

8. Let them fail. Failure is a step to success. It doesn't matter how many times a child falls down as long as they eventually walk, right?

9. Forget about the past. Do not remind your children of misbehavior. But talk frequently of what they did and do well.

10. Take them out often to the store, library, museum, farm, zoo, park, restaurants, malls, story hours, puppet shows etc. The more places your child has been to, the smarter they will be. Many children do poorly in school because they haven't been to

many places and have no frame of reference or exposure to many of the things talked about in their studies.

11. Ask open ended questions that have no single answer which encourage your child to think and explore. Questions like, *"What do you think the dog will do with that toy?"* or *"How did you make the ball bounce so high?"* or even, *"How can you tell if someone is older than you?"*

12. Learning should be fun. Don't embarrass or get angry at your child if they don't know the right answer. Encourage any and all attempts to learn and acknowledge their wrong answers with smiles and a friendly, *"That's close, but not quite right. Try again, you're on the right track."* And if they need a hint, give them one.

13. It isn't helpful to tell a child that something they are struggling with or can't do is easy. Tell them it's hard, but you have faith that they can do it. This way if they fail, it's okay because you said it was hard; and if they get it, they feel twice as good because they figured out something that was hard. If you say it's easy and they don't get it, then they really feel like a failure – anybody can do easy stuff so

they must really be dumb. And if they get it, it's no big deal because it was an easy thing that anyone could do.

14. Ask your child's opinion often and listen. If you don't agree, there is no reason to tell them that they are wrong.

    You could say, *"I don't agree with you because of _____." "Why do you believe_____?"*

    This will encourage a sharing of ideas between you and give you valuable insight into what your child believes and why.

15. As parents, we have three main functions:
    - We are the designers of our child's environment and are responsible for providing a safe, stimulating environment.
    - We are consultants to whom our children can go when they would like advice, need more information or help.
    - We are the final authority, so our child knows who to believe and to trust.

16. When your child makes a grammatical error or mispronounces a word simply rephrase what she

said using correct grammar or pronunciation. For example:

Child: *"I doned it."*
Parent: *"Oh, so you did it."*
Child: *"Look at the Eelephant."*
Parent: *"Yes, I see the elephant."*

This saves the child's face since you are not 'correcting' them, and it models the correct way to say it.

Mealtimes

Mealtime can be especially challenging for parents with young children. To help everyone eat healthy and enjoy mealtimes, follow these simple tips:

1. Ask your child what they like to eat and incorporate these foods into your meals throughout the week.

2. Whenever possible, give the child a choice of two items to pick from. For instance, at breakfast you could ask, "would you like cereal or oatmeal?" Just two choices though. More may overwhelm the child and make it difficult to choose.

3. Having choices increases self-esteem so start this early, around 10 months. If the child can't or won't choose, simply choose for them. If the child asks for something that wasn't one of the choices, you may

provide it if you wish, otherwise say, *"That's not a choice this time. This time you can have* ___ *or* ___, *which is it?"*

4. If your child refuses to eat at mealtime, simply take their plate away and tell them they can eat at the next meal. If it is dinnertime and the child is young (1 to 3 years), you could provide a light snack before bed.

5. If you have to remind or coax your child to eat, you are in a power struggle and giving undue attention to your child. Provide the food, then let the child decide what and how much to eat. No young child has ever willingly refused food often enough to starve.

6. If your child interrupts your conversation at the table, firmly tell them once, *"We are talking, when we are finished it will be your turn."* At the same time raise your index finger. When you finish your comments, then turn to the child and listen to what they have to say. From that point on, do not give the child attention if they interrupt your conversation again. You may raise your index finger as a sign to the child to remain quiet but be sure to turn to the child and listen when it is their turn to talk.

Mealtimes

7. Mealtimes should be relaxing and enjoyable. This is a good time to talk about your child's interests and have a pleasant conversation. This is not the time to discuss poor behavior or to admonish the child for previous wrongdoings.

8. Penelope Leach, the famous child rearing expert, claims that fruits and vegetables have the same vitamins and minerals. Most kids love fruit but hate vegetables. Since this is probably true of your child as well, provide lots of fruit and don't force your child to eat vegetables.

9. It is not advisable to make your child eat foods they don't like. If your child refuses to eat, fine. They can eat at the next meal. How often do you eat food you can't stand? Have the same respect for your child's preferences.

10. Put small helpings on your child's plate and don't require that they eat all the food on their plate. This could cause stress for both you and your child and has been shown to contribute to obesity. Remember too, that a child's stomach is much smaller than an adult's and simply cannot hold as much food.

11. Going out to eat? Remember to bring toys, books, games, paper and pencil or crayons – something to keep the child occupied while waiting for the food and while you eat.

12. Remember to include your child in your mealtime conversations. Some good conversation starters are *"What was the best thing that happened to you at school today? The worst? What was an interesting thing you learned at school? At the park? At scouts? At your friend's house?"* Be sure to share what was the best, worst and interesting thing that happened to you!

At the Grocery Store

Shopping with children under six can be challenging. To make it a pleasant experience for parents and children, follow these simple tips:

1. Make your trip short. 45 minutes maximum unless your child is really interested and behaving well.

2. Be prepared with a list of items you need. This helps keep the trip short and insures you get everything you need in one trip.

3. Before you leave the house tell your child where you are going and what behavior you expect from them. Try not to be too wordy about this. A brief description of the expected behaviors will do.

4. Bring something for your child to do in case they get bored. A favorite toy or book, possibly paper and pencil. This will help avoid behavior problems caused by boredom.

5. As soon as you get a cart, give the child a choice, *"You can walk close to me or sit in the cart, which would you like?"*

6. Children love to be helpers. Let your child pick items for you with your supervision. Things they can handle such as fruits, cereal and canned goods.

7. Be sure to introduce yourself and your child to everyone who works at the store who you deal with. And tell these people how your child is helping you. If they are a baby, comment how they sit so quietly and attentively which helps you shop. This has two great results:

    a. It makes you and your child more social and at ease around others.
    b. Your child will have more reason to behave since people they know are at the store.

8. Show the child the items on your list, sound them out, and point to them in the store. This helps the

child associate written and spoken words with their physical objects.

9. Talk to your child frequently at the store. Point out the variety of food and food groups. Describe what you see on the shelves and ask your child to describe what she sees. This keeps your child's attention focused and helps prevent misbehavior due to boredom. It also stimulates the mind.

10. Ask questions that require the child to think. i.e., *"Point to the cereal we use,"* or *"When do we usually eat cereal?"*

11. Focus on what the child does right and their positive behavior. Describe what they are doing right, such as: *"I really like the way you are walking close to me, thank you. It really helps me when you pick some items too. Then we get done faster. I like shopping with you. I learn so much."*

12. Encourage all attempts at helping and prompt your child in whatever ways will help. For example, if the child is too young to count, point out how many items you need and count for or with the child as he retrieves the items.

13. If the child begins to get into things, you don't want them to, refocus their attention to something else. Perhaps put a box from your cart into their hands and ask questions like, *"What colors do you see in this?"* or *"Is this hard or soft?"* Or ask them to retrieve an item from the shelves for you.

14. If the child refuses to walk close to you, simply put them in the cart and say, *"I see you've decided to sit in the cart."* Then ignore all pleas and cries and talk about other things. Finish your shopping quickly. Tell the child they can try again next time you go shopping. If at the next shopping trip, they misbehave again, go shopping the next time without her. Do not lecture or admonish. Simply tell them you will be going alone this time, and they may try again at the next shopping trip.

15. If the child wants something and you have told them no, then hold firm and do not relent. Saying no and changing it to yes after crying, begging or arguing only leads your child to believe (rightly) that begging and crying will get them what they want. Unless you want a scene every time you shop, make sure that when you say no, you mean it!

At the Grocery Store

16. If your child throws a tantrum and isn't hurting anything, then let them. If it's in the checkout lane, pick up a magazine and read it. Ignore the child. Don't talk to them or look at them. It's your attention they want. If the tantrum is really bad and you just started shopping, go home. You can go to the store later without the child. Do not lecture or admonish the child. They know that what they did was inappropriate. You can tell them how you feel about their behavior, but don't be insulting. A simple, *"I feel annoyed that I couldn't finish my shopping"* or *"I felt embarrassed when you were screaming at the store"* will do. Then drop it. Unless the child brings it up themselves, don't talk about it. Be sure to go shopping without them next time and if they ask, tell them that they can go with you next time. The child will figure out for themselves why you aren't taking them this time, but if they ask, tell them the truth.

17. It if not advisable to promise a treat or reward for good behavior. This is bribery and teaches children to behave well only if there is something in it for them.

18. If your child behaved well during shopping a surprise treat is sometimes in order. You could say

something like: *"Things went so well at the store, and you were so helpful. How about an ice cream cone?"* Or whatever treat you think is appropriate. You determine what would work best with your child. Don't do this every time, or your child will expect a treat every time you go shopping.

19. Don't expect perfect behavior from your children. If you refuse to give up, things will definitely improve. It's as true today as it was a thousand years ago that practice plus patience equals progress. So, Mom and Dad, keep practicing and be patient – you will make progress!

Travel: Across the Street or Across the Country

1. Much misbehavior is caused by boredom. This can easily be avoided. Have toys and books in the car to keep your child occupied while you drive. Bring toys, books, paper and crayons with you to the doctor's office, when visiting friends and family, shopping at department stores and malls and anytime you leave the house.

2. *"Let's count the stop signs... How many red lights will we have?"* or *"How many babies will we see at the mall?"* or *"Let's look for pictures of dogs at the mall."* I think you get the idea. Children are learning machines. These types of activities build their powers of observation while keeping them alert and occupied.

3. Ask open ended questions that have no single answer. These encourage your child to think and explore. Questions like, *"What do you think the dog will do with that bone?"* or *"How did you make your block tower so tall?"*

4. Think before you answer yes or no to your child's requests. Be sure that when you say no, you mean it. Don't change it to a yes if your child whines, cries or argues. This only teaches the child that whining, crying and arguing will get her what she wants.

5. Toddlers can and will play alone, but they must know that you are close by. It is typical for a toddler to stop what they are doing to look for you, and to sit in your lap for a moment or two. This is perfectly normal. They are reassuring themselves that you are there for them. As soon as they're satisfied, they will go back to playing.

6. Notice what your child is doing right and say something about it. For example, *"How nice and quiet you are in the car John, thank you,"* or *"Thank you for being so gentle with little Billy. That's nice of you."*

7. Say nice things about your child to other people and let your child overhear. This really builds

the self-esteem: *"David helped Mary learn to catch today!"* or *"Mary picked up her toys and I didn't even have to ask her!"* Whenever we talk to our son's teachers about him, we always say within his hearing range, *"Anthony is such a pleasure. We're lucky to have him."*

8. If your child acts up in the car, simply pull over and calmly tell your child that you will resume driving **AS SOON AS** they are quiet and strapped in their seat. Keep a book or magazine in the car to keep you occupied as you wait for the child(ren) to behave. The first time you do this, the kids will be shocked! And your first car trip using this technique may require several stops as the children test whether you mean it or not. I guarantee that if you do this calmly, not as a means of punishment, and if you keep quiet, the children will behave perfectly. Even the unruliest children will be tamed by the third or fourth car ride.

9. Some children will not wear their seatbelt or they will unbuckle it while you are driving. If they do not put it on before you start driving, simply do not start driving. Be sure to keep books and magazines in the car to keep you busy as you wait for their compliance. If they unbuckle as you drive, pull

over to a safe place and wait for compliance before driving. Remind them it is against the law to drive with an unbuckled child in the car.

Creating a Safe Home

Just like the major car manufacturer's ad says, *"Safety is Job #1!"* Especially when we have children in the home. For safety's sake, it's a good idea to see your house from the perspective of your children.

To see your home from a baby or toddler's point of view, get down on your hands and knees and slowly crawl around observing all the potential safety hazards accessible to your child that you haven't thought of before. Things like the heavy glass candy dish on the coffee table. The sharp corners on the tables and chairs. Lighters or matches within reach of precious little hands. Small pieces of lint and dirt that crawling babies always seem to find and put in their mouths, noses and ears. Small parts from your older children's toys. Pens, pencils and crayons. Hot food. Cords dangling from coffee pots and small appliances that invite disasters.

Yes, You Can

Our children depend on us to keep them safe. Here are a few tips to help you create a safe home:

1. Use the back burners of the stove when you cook. Be sure to turn the pot handles toward the back of the stove, not the front where a child could grab it and cause a potentially fatal accident.

2. Put a gate up to keep your child out of the kitchen when you aren't in it. There are many fine spring-loaded gates which fit tightly. Check that your child cannot climb over the gate or push it down. Keep the age of your child in mind when blocking stairs. A child under 18 months should only be allowed to climb up two to three stairs on their own.

3. Prepare a safe cabinet in the kitchen for your baby or toddler to play in while you cook and wash dishes. Fill a lower cabinet with safe plastic or *Tupperware* bowls, cups, lids etc. Your child will play happily and safely while you work. Be sure to compliment your child, *"You are playing so nicely and quietly. I'm glad you are here with me."*

4. Put cleaners and detergents on top shelves and sharp objects in locked drawers. Buy cabinet locks to keep your child safe from all harmful substances

Creating a Safe Home

and objects. Cabinet locks are inexpensive and easy to install.

5. Keep all cords out of your child's reach. Keep the cords to the rear of tables and desks and close to the wall. Buy cord holders which cover and hold cords along the wall. Plug all exposed outlets with child proof plugs.

6. Never leave a child under four years of age in the bathtub alone. They could drown in as little as two inches of water, or they could accidently turn on the hot water and scald themselves. Unfortunately, these completely preventable tragedies have happened many times.

   If you have infants or children under three (3) years of age, get down on your hands and knees and crawl through your home to spot any potential dangers.

*Children raised with **respect** and **cooperation** are likely to be **respectful** and **cooperative**.*

To Strengthen Your Marriage

Children can strain even the best marriage. We must set rules and limits on our children's behavior in order to help preserve the basic relationship of the family – that between a husband and wife. If physical or verbal abuse are not involved, preservation of the marriage should be of primary importance.

1. Establish your children's bedtime to be at least one hour before you and your spouse go to bed. You two need time alone everyday, if possible.

2. Write **KNOCK** in very large letters on a piece of paper and hang it on the outside of your bedroom door, at your child's eye level. If your children are two and one half or older, explain to them what it

says and that when the door is closed, they must knock and wait for you to say *"come in"* before opening the door. Then rehearse. Go into the room and close the door. Have the child knock. Rehearse both *"come in"* and *"Stay out, Mommy and Daddy will be out in a little while."* Praise your child for his reading ability and how well he knocks and follows directions. Be sure to practice this every so often so your child remembers to knock when your door is closed.

3. Do not disagree with your spouse's decisions regarding discipline in front of the children. This makes it too easy for the children to divide and conquer the two of you. Talk to your spouse in private and find mutually acceptable ways to discipline the children.

4. Do not permit yourself or your spouse to physically or verbally abuse your children. Your children must know someone will protect them from harm and you or your spouse must learn that in loving families there is a line we do not cross.

5. Learn to be a good listener. A good listener just listens. Let your partner know you are listening with a few well-placed 'oohs' and 'ahhs'. Don't give

advice unless asked. Even then I reply, *"I'm not sure dear. What do you think?"*

6. Do whatever is necessary to be sure you and your spouse get an evening out alone together at least once a month. Plan this ahead of time and make sure you do it. Romantic relationships require opportunities to feel romantic, unstressed and to be alone together. As hard as it may be to remember now, you were lovers before you became parents.

7. Compliment your spouse every day. Let him or her know how important they are to you and how much you love them. *"You are so attractive. I am so happy to be married to YOU. You are such a patient, caring mother/father."* We all need to know we are loved and what is lovable about us.

8. Thank your spouse for the everyday things he or she does. *"It means a lot to me that you take out the garbage without ever being asked,"* or *"I appreciate that you go to work every day,"* or even, *"I like the way you spend time with the children and take them with you when you run errands."*

9. Ask your spouse to help you rather than demand it. No one likes to be ordered around.

10. Speak well of your in-laws and your spouse's friends. Find what you like about them. No one likes to hear bad things about their family all the time. We all like to hear good things about our families and friends.

11. Let your parents and in-laws spoil your children if they like. Let their relationship with them be just that – their relationship. It is only parents who are really unsure of their own parenting skills who insist that everyone else treat their children the same way they do. You probably act differently with your boss than with your spouse. That's because they expect different behaviors from you. Your children learn quickly, too, that they can act one way with grandma and another with you. It isn't confusing – it's life. Don't attempt to change anyone's behavior but your own. Everyone will be much happier that way.

Children need:
- **P**rotection
- **A**ttention
- **R**ules
- **E**ncouragement
- fu**N**
- conversa**T**ion
- firm limit**S**

Yes, You Can

Remember

- I have the courage to be imperfect. I do what I believe is right for my children and do not concern myself with what other people may think.

- When I say no, I mean it. When I say yes, I mean it.

- I expect the best and I am prepared for the worst.

- I allow my child to say no to me sometimes.

- To avoid problems, I use **AS SOON AS**. "**As soon as** your toys are picked up, you can go outside to play."

- I notice the **good** and say something about it **every day**.

- I apologize to my child when I am wrong.

- I ask my children to help, rather than always tell them to.

- I give my child choices every day and I honor their preferences.

- I notice my child's assets and strengths and comment on them.

- I hug my child and say, *"I love you"* everyday.

- I encourage my child to think of solutions before I give advice.

- I never use teasing, sarcasm or name calling. These have no place in loving relationships.

- I say please and thank you to my child.

- I tell my child what I do want, rather than what I don't want.

Yes, You Can

There is a big difference between praise and encouragement. Praise actually discourages and makes children believe they are only worthy when they are achieving something or doing something adults want them to. It is a form of social control.

Praise:

Definition: Praise is the expression of approval, commendation, or admiration for a person's achievements, qualities, or behavior.

Praise is like saying, *"Good job!"* when someone does well. It's when we tell someone they're smart, or the best at something. Praise is about celebrating the end result, like getting an A+ on a test or being the star player on a team.

Characteristics:

1. **Outcome-Focused:** Praise often emphasises the end result or the accomplishment itself.
2. **External Validation:** It provides external affirmation and recognition.
3. **Generalised Statements:** Praise may be more general, highlighting the overall success rather than specific aspects.
4. **Fixed Mindset:** Constant praise for innate abilities can unintentionally foster a fixed mindset, where individuals believe their abilities are static.

Yes, You Can

Examples:

- *"Great job on getting an A+ in the test!"*
- *"You're so smart!"*
- *"You're the best player on the team!"*

Encouragement:

Definition: Encouragement is the expression of support, confidence, and motivation to inspire someone to continue their efforts or overcome challenges.

Encouragement is more like cheering someone on. It's saying, *"I see you working hard,"* or *"I believe you can do it!"*

Encouragement focuses on the effort and progress, not just the final result. It's about helping someone feel confident and motivated to keep trying, even if things are a bit tough.

Characteristics:

1. **Process-Focused:** Encouragement often emphasises the effort, progress, or strategies used in the pursuit of a goal.
2. **Internal Motivation:** It aims to build internal motivation and self-confidence.

3. **Specific Feedback:** Encouragement is often more specific, highlighting particular efforts or improvements.
4. **Growth Mindset:** It fosters a growth mindset by emphasising the belief that abilities can be developed through effort and learning.

Examples:

- *"I can see how hard you worked on that assignment. Your effort really shows!"*
- *"You're facing a challenge, but I believe in your ability to figure it out."*
- *"It's okay if you didn't win this time. What matters is that you tried your best, and I'm proud of your effort."*

The Main Differences Between Praise and Encouragement

While both praise and encouragement can be positive, encouragement tends to focus more on the process, effort and growth mindset. It provides constructive feedback, motivates individuals to persevere, and helps build resilience.

Praise, on the other hand, often centers on the outcome or innate qualities, and while it can boost confidence, it may not offer as much guidance for improvement or the development of a growth mindset. The key is to strike a balance and use a combination of both approaches to support and uplift individuals effectively.

In short, praise is like a high-five for doing well, while encouragement is more like a supportive coach, cheering you on no matter what, and helping you get better along the way.

Both are good, but encouragement is often like a friend helping you through challenges and celebrating your progress!

About The Author

Martha Burich, author of *Yes You Can Raise Happy, Responsible Children*, brings over two decades of experience in education and psychology to her work. With 10 years as a college psychology professor and 16 years as a high school science teacher, as well as a background in special education, she possesses a deep understanding of human behavior and learning.

Armed with a master's degree plus in education and a passion for empowering others, Martha Burich has dedicated her career to helping individuals and families thrive. Her presentations and trainings reflect her commitment to sharing insights gleaned from years of studying behavior change.

Through her book, Martha combines academic expertise with real-world experience to provide practical strategies for fostering happy, responsible children. Drawing from her rich background in education and psychology, she offers valuable guidance that resonates with parents, educators and caregivers alike.

As a dynamic speaker and advocate for positive change, Martha has been a show host and continues to be a popular guest on podcasts and shows. She continues to inspire audiences with her knowledge, compassion and unwavering belief in the potential of every individual.

Resources

Cooperative Discipline. Linda Albert Circle Pines, MN. AGS 1991

Homecoming: Reclaiming and Championing Your Inner Child. John Bradshaw New York: Bantam Books, 1990.

How to Talk so Kids Will Listen and Listen so Kids Will Talk. Adele Faber and Elaine Mazlish New York: Rawson 1980.

How to be a No Limit Person. Wayne Dyer New York: William Morrow & Co. 1989.

The Parents Handbook: Systematic Training for Effective Parenting. Don Dinkmeyer & Gary McKay. Circle Pines, NM: AGS 1982.

Savage Spawn: Reflections on Violent Children. Jonathan Kellerman. New York, NY: Random House 1999

52 Things Kids Need From A Dad. Jay Payleitner. Eugene, OR: Harvest House 2010

Supernanny: How to Get the Best From Your Children. Jo Frost. New York, NY: Hyperion 2005

The Out-of Sync Child: Recognizing and Coping With Sensory Integration Dysfunction. Carol Stock Kranowitz. New York, NY: Skylight Press 1998

The Explosive Child. Ross W. Greene. New York, NY: HarperCollins 2021

Healthy Parenting. Janet G. Woititz. New York, NY: Simon & Schuster 1992

Positive Parenting From A to Z. Karen Renshaw Joslin. New York, NY: Ballantine Books 1994

The Optimistic Child. Martin E.P. Seligman. New York, NY: Houghton Mifflin 2007

The Psychology of the Child. Jean Piaget and Barbara Inhelder. New York, NY: Basic Books 1969

What Do You Really Want For Your Children? Wayne Dyer. New York, NY: Avon Books 1985

A New Guide to Rational Living. Albert Ellis, Robert Harper. Englewood Cliffs, NJ: Prentice-Hall 1975

Offers

Please accept this free gift as
a thank you for purchasing this book.

An article I wrote with information to
help you change your life now:

**https://mailchi.mp/marthaburich/
how-to-change-your-life-now**

Join my free private Facebook group to see videos and interact with other parents and caregivers here:

**https://www.facebook.com/
share/1rodCeYmTQYCqgFB/**

www.ingramcontent.com/pod-product-compliance
Lightning Source LLC
Chambersburg PA
CBHW030311100526
44590CB00012B/593